Frailties

The Subtle Art of Falling Apart

Anirudh Das

India | USA | UK

Made with ❤ on the BookLeaf Publishing Platform
www.bookleafpub.in
www.bookleafpub.com

Dedication

Like sprawling stars guide a lost pilgrim to his destination, I dedicate this collection to everyone in my life who has shown me the right path whenever I falter.

Preface

Frailties makes me ponder over the mortality of human shackles and the immortality of soul. No matter how forsaken or derelict one's retrospection highlights, it's very hard to come in terms with one's own self rather than facing those forces which cater impediments in our path.This poem showcases not only the emotional turmoil when one comes face to face with his/her own self and their past but also provide a vivid portrayal of last stand against the totalitarian surroundings which govern the every faculty of life.

Acknowledgements

I would like to express my heartfelt gratitude to my family, friends and readers for their encouragement and honest feedback.A special thanks to Book Leaf Publication for offering a platform to expend my suppressed thoughts and emotions. This book would not have been possible without you all.

1. Fallen Angel

A semblance overflowed with serenity,
A presence with divine affinity,
An eclipse to every distraught around,
A fallen angel tethered to the earthly bound.

Such ethereal beauty once trod the firmament,
Envy of unworthy angels fuelled their lament.
A mere angel who made the God kneel,
To forsake whom; underwent devil's deal
.

Forgotten and cursed; yet undeterred,
So magnanimous, yet had immortality severed,
A daffodil bright as sun in a frigid womb,
Trapped in an concocted eternal loom.

Corrugation unknown to humble temple,
Unscarred chastity of everlasting dimple.

2. Till Death do Us Apart

Shivers across the contorted vine,
Succumbed to otiose; a torpor soul,
But an impalpable gaze of such a divine,
An awry conscience started to become whole.

Creeping through the unholy icy veins,
A throb; forgotten in wallows of past,
Undulating yet still trapped in inevitable chains,
Resisting immortality; just to break a perpetual fast.

Laurels of angels beckon the stubborn soul,
Unheeded to quintessential muses seven,
Concerned for his Hera in white stole,
Sniffles tugs remnant off the heaven.

Severed off life; devoid of any sensate; an impending dusk,
Yearns to once again feel through the fading husk.

3. Given

Reprimanded for being part of you,
A desolate cry heard by few.
Incarcerated agonies of past seep,
Enough to make Noah's ark creak.

 Uncouth slurs pangs, deprived society choke,
But your scent makes it difficult to cope.
Revisiting trodden path through memory lane,
Disappearing imprints leaves the present in pain.

Phantom of past satiates the emptiness of soul,
Enigmatic over fabrication from unearthly toll.
Stream of time can perish and make everything anew,
Yet fail to wither the regret of never saying I LOVE
YOU.

4. A Failure's Dilemma

Afloat by the still waters,
A Nederland where not a feather flutters.
Fading conscience hails for delusional salvation,
 A promised haven devoid of all anticipation.

 Hunger for an ambient posterity,
Led to forsake the tepid pleasures of reality.
Meretricious utopia allures the gullible,
Tethers of souls so easily sellable.

Every bond dilutes since transience pollutes,
Farcical world full of sniffling dews.
Unchained valour of living lulled back to sleep,
Such far-fetched dreams corrugates into rubbish heap.

What is it! But a cry of a fallen, villain, rogue, thief,
Severed from godhood, over an apple; a divine cleave.
Floating away on still currents to unknown,
A scent of relief over failure's won.

5. Alone

Scorching pangs of desolate wonderland,
Plunged in cacophony of passivity and despair.
Succumbed from a sudden strand,
A sully soul about which no one care.

Innocent soul longs for closure,
Yet showered with haughty gaze.
The era to indulge in maternal pleasure,
Faded and brimming with scathing haze.

A genteel touch dispelled all the passivity,
Drought stricken ravine flooded through valley of naught.
 Ray of light shines the crevices of pity,
Soon the warmth froze and left with broken knot.

Bud longs for the lost light,
Ignorant fool fall for the radiance of firefly.
Tries to bloom like a clipped bird ventures for flight,
Last strand of life withers before the recognition of lie.

6. Apart

Ashes smothering the lifeless soul,
As a melancholic embrace of a stranded lover.
A desperate measure to become whole,
Crumbling hope accentuates as the inevitable hover.

Sinking into the pit of abysmal despair,
The famine struck the Eden
As no one left for the apple to share.

Concepts wither passivity succumbs from broken knot,
Cursed with pangs of thirst yet rejects to cure
Soul void of warmth and care commence to rot.

Decimated spirit longs for that sensual touch,
Longs to once again bathe in tranquil gaze.
And slips in search nostalgic persona of such,
Just to again revert back to good old days.

7. Amazon

A Celestial grace from the land of Gods,
A being to teach humans trod.
Soul blessed with embers of sun,
Warmth of which can be seen in her pun.

Defiled and ravaged by destiny,
Yet with stern eyes she faces such mutiny.
Scars which keep her awake all night,
Her colossal will refuses to give up without a fight.

Every day she is reminded of destiny's heist,
Jealousy towards her gifts made it so biased.
I hail O foolish destiny haven't you yet realized.
Who thought you to be so surmised?

Every envious infliction of your chaos,
Have made your authority over her otiose.
O pitiful destiny your whips made her iron maiden,
She had eluded your treacherous heathen.

You don't even scare her anymore,
Thanks to you, she would soon soar.
Like a fledgling leaving her nest beyond the firmament,
She can reach the heights beyond your discernment.

8. Old-Age

A quaint shade whispers out in glee,
A lap, once a cradle, now you flee,
Grief-stricken vines cluttered around,
A cry of birth none can unsound.

As autumn sets and brittle bones clatter,
No poet glorifies a glass that shatter,
Human speaks beast; beast speaks none,
Replete altars under the eclipsed sun.

A rivulet meanders through forgotten woods,
Unseen kingdom, unknown to returning hoods,
Such suzerainty calls for deserving deed,
What forebodings one didn't heed?

9. A Girl Next Door

Like a flower blooms in candid spring morning,
Such smile she carries every morning.
The word "beautiful" describes many things,
Yet fall short to define her soul with wings.

A pretty and ethereal goddess of heaven,
Tumbled down in this hell in year 1997.
Trounced and chastised by so-called cultural society,
Idol worship, religious war and a world of false piety.

A divine being in this cursed world, full of invalids,
A blessing, born to turn them into valids.
I refrain the world to possess such a being,
Only mine she is, yet I dare not say deign.

Spirit of Themistocles resides in petite human denture,
A bare warrior trodding alone, a perilous venture.

10. Dystopian Utopia

A covert glance peering through horizon,
In hope to get utopian provision.
None play martyr more skilfully,
Than a neighbour,hillbilly.

A viscous grey matter; derelict and unread.
Following a creed like gregarious undead.
Frolicking over the hunger unfazed,
An oppressed freedom left none amazed.

None so well-versed; a savant of beggary
Too affected and conceited to indulge in drudgery.
Strides of gazelle, a delusion of every limp,
Could such feat be matched by a blind pimp?

Cruel is destiny to subject gullible fools,
In front of a savage that drools.
So lively and so patriotic; trudge in mirth high,
A forbidden hope to rob sun of lifeless sky.

11. Adolescence

Clamour! Clamour! Clamour!
As they run their tongues without stammer,
Giggling away,unknown of what to come,
A smite of destiny; made them forget to hum.

Sterile is their soul; untainted by time
Soon they enter a world where they worth a dime.
Forgotten; once there were days so sublime.

Striding away in the bliss of moment,
Undeterred by the burning compartment.
Stench of burning flesh; doesn't wake the dreamer
An eternal slumber as illusion gets more gleamer.

Ripples of time; its contemporary insignificance,
Wreck havoc; flushed out, good riddance.
Ethunized philosophies of all apostles
Foreshadows the truth, till all are fossils
O! Nature, why you hide your thistle,
To raise innocence on a cracked pedestal.

12. Salary-man

A brown strapped satchel, full of wear and tear,
Walking off with distilled vision and will in gear,
Along came the gentry with stories unknown,
While himself misty and blurred bonds of one's own.

Trivialized depression which one shall not express,
An anomaly which could make loyalties digress.
Slithering snakes coiling around the foolish idealist,
Sucking out his scorching vigour, turning him into
nihilist.

Trampled and suffocated with no respite to breathe,
"To be true to oneself"- what a heinous deed.
An army of dead breathes and speaks among us,
Many nonchalant about the blood they gush.

Why broken bones and torn tendon kept hush?
Always disguised to hide a face full of pus.
No cell unmoved when the bell tolls 12:00,
Sprawling concrete anthills where no soul dwell.

13. Let Bygones be Bygones

Time resonates every scintilla across,
Skipped beat on every roundabout and cross.
Uphill and winding roads of life,
Ignorant to such divinity my intellect naive.

Cynical self of mine bloated with doubt,
How Eden on barren could sprout.
What moons, suns and stars but inert,
What even fame, wealth or life worth.

Everything outsourced by your aura around,
A lost shepherd found by an anklet's sound.
Flow of time none can yet reverse
To alert ghosts of past how to traverse

Too late to start a journey anew,
Every heartache is happy just to see you.

14. Mirror

Surrendered vigour under the caustic hate,
No more could fathom the stitched fate.
Once frolicking hues under the surreal sun,
Harrowing shade now envelopes a pious nun.
Ingenuous memories sizzle away into air,.
Corrugated phlegm strips the vocals bare

Narrow glen drowned under majestic boulder,
Forlorn and abandoned none left to shoulder
Cursed to enjoy mirth in embezzled love
A botched nature which preys on cautious dove.
Shattered and tattered; adieu to molested innocence
Embers seethe through carcass; to undue diligence.

An invalid is born, uncouth enough to forsake bevy
No unjust justice could indulge his conscience levy.
Idyllic tethers withers like snow in windy afternoon,
Trapped in the web on one's own fabricated moon.
A parade of souls wallow under the tyrant's thumb,
Once a sensitive soul; now every scintilla turned numb.

15. Time

Tick - Tock the clock goes on,
Perturbed with life, inevitable is born.

Immortality recedes from shores of humanity,
Foreboding clouds ravishes virgin serenity.

Newfangled claws of gluttonous greed,
Allures its prey to do heinous deed.

Flock once unknown to envy and despair,
Blinded with rage and forsaken what to care.

Brethren once humble; now full of conceit,
New Era devoid of love; well-versed to cheat.

Innocent betrayal made gazillions mourn,
Tick - Tock the clock goes on.

16. Lost Soul

Prattle of past yearns for peace,
Tranquil of present need it in lease.

Distant future unknown of itself,
Hesitate to comprehend himself.

Eclipsed dawn after the swarthy night,
Perpetual dusk wrought by divine might.

Nightmares fuel today with dreams,
Insomnia recalls those nights with gleam.

Everlasting promises are forsaken,
Audacity of love why so mistaken?

Loneliness fulfills one's void of closure,
Despair, a friend before eternal foreclosure.

17. The Illusion of Life

Zest of frolicking hues after rain,
Dazzling beacon of light left in vain.

Such forlorn tears of ethereal nature,
Bestow mortals a visual treat of this stature.

Exponential exploitation of damsel estranged,
Every offspring gnawed her chastity deranged.

The pinnacle of maternal sacrifice falter,
Witnessed atrocities would make wombs deter.

Concocted desires gauging the scars of life,
A wonderland of delusion; an eternal dive.

Yet salvation nowhere to be found,
A devil's curse every human is bound.

Revisiting down the memory lane,
Escaping as present is hard to tame.

Hoping to find solace in crevices of past,
To find hope or a reason to last.

Every echelon resonates to the desperate call,
Like an unnerved pupil of academic hall.

Echoes of uncharted mysteries left undone,
Lesions sealed envelopes the crippled sun.

Perpetual marathon left the future awry,
Every mile is a step away from glory.

O foolish traveler! Heed to caution of mine,
You need to cross the starting line.

18. Forbidden Love

Snowy petals foster glimpses forsaken,
Flattered moments left mistaken.
Follies treacherous to enigmatic life,
Solved the mysteries for this lost naive.

Felicity over the heinous immorality,
Moral compass true to undying fidelity.
A night sky devoid of any star,
Subsumes the darkness from afar.

Distorted past starts to unwind,
Nothing left in future to find.
Voracious search for truth of life,
True answers are never suffice.

Undulating breathes become shadier,
Zenith can only be found at nadir.

19. A Curse called Love

Soaring across the fleeting horizon,
Utopian traveler succumbed to poison.

Drooling dew off the bashful leaf,
Cautious buds whom thirsty bees peeve.

A virulent plague merciless in nature
A cure of which is unknown to creature.

Every symptom of which brings dismay,
Illustrated illusions trap the gullible prey.

Convalescence of which led to otiose,
No one is immune to its visceral chaos.

Sardonic pleasure lies in desolation,
A disease of man's own creation.

Intoxication to pain left conscience awake,
Caricature scant from nectar but heartache.

20. On the Way to Glory

As the sun peeps through the horizon,
Over my reeking sweat which remained undone.
As my body locked in the armor,
Like the hug of a perishing lover.

My hand clenches tightly the sword,
On the sight of the battlefield full of rival horde.
Seeing the might of the enemy swells my heart,
Not of my hopelessness; the thought that my friends
may drift apart.

We grew, played, cried together out loud,
Thousand stakes riddles the heart on seeing them in
celestial shroud.
Savages skirmished them like dark figure,
Strength of Hercules leaked off their vigour.

Drought has struck the land from the ferociousness of
war,
Whose thirst is not of rain but the blood is now its cure.

The anger of dejection can be felt from the hot whips of
nature,
It reminds the kisses of Utopian angel over my cheeks
before departure.

With every moment's death the shiver swaps the throb,
Over an inevitable ponder that free souls can make loved
ones sob.
The glimpse of home stammers the spirit; dismal sword's
shine,
As now the doors to immortality is separated by a thin
red line.

The wandering through the bewitched meadows of past,
Aids the deteriorating conscience and draws a vivid
picture for what to last.
As the adrenaline kicks off the will, my sword rises in
the front trajectory,
With the withering oblivion, eyes are stern for the grasp
of victory.

21. Despair

Frigid caricature full of flesh and wine,
Dither to live; busy to cry; a stilted mime.
Hopeless, yet hopeful for destined fate,
Ghosts of past left with unquenched hate.

Prattle of rain soaks not the flesh but soul,
Empty carcass drowned in abysmal hole.
Woods devoid of fauna; trees without leaves,
A dystopian wonderland our deed weaves.

Book of life full of morbid twists and turn,
Every chapter ends with pity and yearn.
Fragile yet tenacious being tethers to reality,
Ripples of past filled them with depravity.

Despondence lulls the conscience to sleep,
Muffled tears invisible to peep.
Tumultuous oblivion devoid of peace,
Every scintilla demands to void the lease.

War broke leaving the scathes victorious,
Battered will left the impending future treacherous.
Cold winds o forlorn utopia alleviates the fire,
Past follies are what groggy spirits admire.

No path of repentance for the unspoken,
Delusional self yet to be awoken..